GEORGE BUSH
Forty-First President of the United States

By June Behrens

CP CHILDRENS PRESS®

CHICAGO

Inauguration of President George Bush and Vice President Dan Quayle at the U.S. Capitol, January 20, 1989. President Bush and Mrs. Bush walk down Pennsylvania Avenue (opposite page).

To my Mother, Aline York

Library of Congress Cataloging-in-Publication Data

Behrens, June.
  George Bush: The forty-first president of the United
States / by June Behrens.
    p.   cm. — (Picture story biography)
  Summary: Examines the life and career of the man who
served as vice-president of the United States for eight years
under Ronald Reagan and was then elected to follow him as
the forty-first president.
  ISBN 0-516-04172-X
  1. Bush, George, 1924-   —Juvenile
literature.   2.   Presidents—United States—Biography—
Juvenile literature.   [1.   Bush, George,
1924-   2.   Presidents.] I. Title. II. Series.
E882.B44   1989
973.928'092'4—dc19   89-693
[B]   CIP
[92]   AC

HAIL TO THE CHIEF! Bands
played and people cheered their new
president. George Bush had taken
the oath of office. He was now the
forty-first president of the United
States. A grand parade followed the
inauguration on January 20, 1989.

George and Barbara Bush live in
the White House. They have a

summer home in Kennebunkport, Maine. George Bush is at home in many states. He was born in Massachusetts. He grew up in Connecticut. He lives in Washington. But he calls Texas his home.

The Bush summer home in Kennebunkport, Maine, is at Walker Point. The Kennebunk River is at the top of the picture.

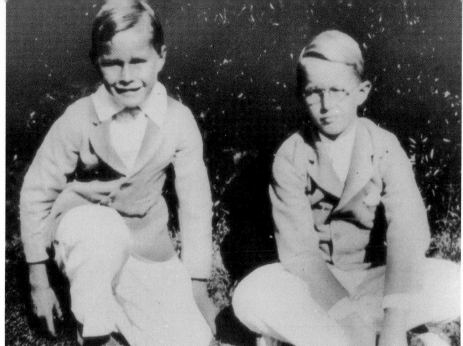

George as a toddler (left) and with his older brother Prescott (right)

Dorothy Walker Bush named her second son George Herbert Walker Bush after her father. Prescott and Dorothy Bush lived in Massachusetts. George was born there in 1924. The family later settled in Connecticut. George grew up with his three brothers and a sister in Greenwich, Connecticut.

George remembers happy summer days at Walker's Point in Kennebunkport, Maine. This was Grandfather Walker's home.

George learned to love the sea on
this rocky Maine coast. Grandfather
Walker taught his grandchildren
how to fish. He showed them
how to handle a boat. They learned
the mysteries of tidepool life.

George was called "Poppy" in
those early days. He was named
Poppy after Grandfather Walker,
who was called "Pop."

When he finished at Greenwich
Country Day School, George
entered prep school. At Phillips
Academy in Andover,
Massachusetts, George made his
mark in sports. He was captain of the
basketball and soccer teams. He
played baseball. George was elected
president of his senior class. He was
voted the "most respected"
member of his class.

George was graduated from
Phillips Academy in 1942. That

At Phillips Academy in Andover, Massachusetts (below), George played baseball (upper left) and took part in student activities (upper right), such as book drives for the loan library.

Ensign George Bush (left) was assigned to the *U.S.S. San Jacinto* (above).

summer, on the day he turned 18, George enlisted in the Navy. He trained in Corpus Christi, Texas, and became a junior officer. Ensign George Bush was the youngest pilot in the United States Navy.

The United States was in the middle of World War II. Ensign George Bush was assigned to the aircraft carrier *U.S.S. San Jacinto*. He flew torpedo bombers in combat missions over the Pacific Ocean for a year and a half.

Torpedo bomber, launched from the *U.S.S. San Jacinto*, flies over Majuro Atoll in the Marshall Islands on May 30, 1944.

Distinguished Flying Cross

On September 2, 1944, George Bush was shot down while on a bombing mission. He parachuted from the plane into the Pacific Ocean and floated in a rubber raft until he was rescued by a submarine. George Bush was awarded the Distinguished Flying Cross. He returned home a hero.

George Bush served in the United States Navy from 1942 to 1945. At the time he left the service, George was Lieutenant Bush.

Barbara and George dance at their wedding.

What a wonderful Christmas 1944! Lieutenant Bush was home with his family in Greenwich. Two weeks later he married his sweetheart, Barbara Pierce. She was a student at Smith College. They were married at her family church in Rye, New York.

George played on the Yale University baseball team.

After the war, George Bush
returned to school. He entered Yale
University and three years later he
earned a degree in economics. An
honor student, George was elected
to Phi Beta Kappa, an honor society.
George Bush was an outstanding
athlete at Yale. He was captain of the
baseball team and played first base.
He would never forget meeting the

George and his hero Babe Ruth.

famous home-run hitter, "Babe" Ruth, during his senior year.

The year 1948 was a big one for Barbara and George Bush. George was now a graduate of Yale. He decided not to join his father's Wall Street firm. Instead, George and Barbara would seek their fortune out west, in Texas.

Odessa, Texas, in the early 1950s

George, Barbara, and their young son George settled in west Texas. They lived in Odessa near the oil fields. George started working as a laborer, sweeping warehouses and painting rigs. He later became a drilling-tools salesman. George learned every part of the oil business.

15

In 1950, the Bush family, including young George and his little sister Robin, moved to Midland, Texas. The family settled into a little house on Easter Egg Row. George Bush remembers that this was the time and place for ambitious young families.

George and a friend, John Overby, started a business in oil and gas properties. By 1953 they joined the Liedtke brothers to form a new company. It was named Zapata Petroleum Corporation. George Bush was 30 years old when he co-founded this company.

In the next year, the Zapata Offshore Company was founded as a part of the Zapata Corporation. The company developed offshore drilling equipment. George Bush became the company's president.

George Bush at a 1957 meeting of the Desk & Derrick Club of Midland, Texas.

The Bush family suffered a
personal tragedy during these years.
Robin, their beautiful three-year-
old daughter, died of leukemia.
George did not give in to his grief.
He was back teaching Sunday school
in Midland a week later. The loss of
Robin is an ache George and
Barbara Bush have said they will
carry with them always.

The Bush family: George, Jr., George, Barbara. Standing in front of Mrs. Bush are John, Neil, and Marvin, the youngest boy.

In 1959 the Zapata business was split. George Bush, president of Zapata Offshore Company, moved his family and company headquarters to Houston. The offshore drilling business became very successful.

The young Bush family had gone to Texas to seek their fortune. They had found it. And how the family had grown! Along with young George were three brothers, John, Neil, and Marvin, and a sister, Dorothy.

18

Senator Prescott Sheldon Bush (left). George and Barbara leave the voting booth in 1964. He lost this election to the U.S. Senate.

George Bush had enjoyed a successful business career. Now he was interested in public service. Perhaps he thought of his father. Senator Prescott Bush had served the state of Connecticut for 10 years.

Taking a leave of absence from his business, Bush ran for the U.S. Senate on the Republican ticket. He captured 43.5 percent of the vote. That was a very good result for a Republican in Texas in 1964.

However, Bush lost the Senate race to Democrat Ralph W. Yarborough.

Two years later George Bush ran for office again. This time he won a seat in the U.S. House of Representatives. Congressman Bush was reelected for a second term. He represented Texas' Seventh Congressional district from 1967 to 1971.

George Bush tried again for the Senate seat in 1970. He lost to Democrat Lloyd M. Bentsen, Jr.

In 1966 George was elected to the U.S. House of Representatives. In 1970 George ran for the U.S. Senate against Lloyd M. Bentsen, Jr. (far right) and lost.

President Richard M. Nixon (third from the left) asked George Bush to represent the United States at the United Nations. U.N. Secretary General U Thant (right) welcomed Ambassador Bush (right).

In Washington, Congressman Bush made many friends. President Nixon liked his work. He named George Bush the United States Ambassador to the United Nations.

Two years later President Nixon called George Bush back to Washington. He named Bush chairman of the Republican National Committee. Bush served the party for more than a year.

George Bush walks with Lin Ping, Director of the Department of American and Oceanic Affairs for the People's Republic of China.

When Gerald Ford became president, Bush was given a new job. President Ford asked him to represent the United States in the People's Republic of China. George and Barbara Bush then moved to Beijing, China.

President Ford needed George Bush. After a year in China, George and Barbara were returned home.

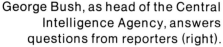
George Bush, as head of the Central
Intelligence Agency, answers
questions from reporters (right).

The president appointed George
Bush Director of the Central
Intelligence Agency. As head of the
CIA, Bush made changes that
improved future operations of the
agency.

George Bush left the CIA when
Jimmy Carter became president.

In 1979 George Bush announced he intended to seek the Republican presidential nomination. He lost the nomination to Ronald Reagan.

By 1979 George Bush had been in public service for 15 years. He had taken many leadership roles. Now he was seeking the biggest job of all, president of the United States.

George Bush hit the campaign trail. He crisscrossed the nation. He worked hard for the Republican party nomination. Ronald Reagan of California also wanted the job.

George Bush (left), former President Gerald Ford (center), and Ronald Reagan (right) at the Republican convention in 1980.

Ronald Reagan won the Republican nomination for president in July 1980. Reagan selected George Bush as his running mate. Bush became the vice presidential nominee. The election was four months away. They had work to do. The Reagan-Bush team won. They served for eight years as president and vice president of the United States.

25

11333-95

From the beginning President
Reagan gave Vice President Bush
important jobs. From his office in
the White House, Bush led a crisis
team, working to solve national
problems. He was chairman of many
committees. Vice President Bush
helped with decisions in foreign
affairs.

While President Ronald Reagan was recovering from a gunshot wound, Vice President Bush ran the cabinet meetings (left). Prime Minister Zenko Suzuki and a guard of honor (right) welcomed Vice President Bush to Japan in 1982.

George Bush was there when the president could not be present. He traveled hundreds of thousands of miles. In meetings across the nation, Bush represented the president. He met with world leaders. He attended inaugurations, funerals, and state affairs representing the United States.

In 1988 George Bush campaigned in Orlando, Florida (above left), Boston, Massachusettes (above right), and San Antonio, Texas (below). He won the support of people throughout the United States.

From left to right: Barbara and George Bush, Dan and Marilyn Quayle
with their daughter Corinne

In 1988 George Bush ran for the
office of president. He was warmly
endorsed by President Reagan.
George Herbert Walker Bush won
the election on November 8, 1988.
He was one of the most experienced
men ever elected. He would be "at
home" in the White House.

This official White House photograph shows President and Mrs. Bush surrounded by their children and their grandchildren.

President Bush works long hours. But he always finds time for his large family of five grown children and ten grandchildren. His mother, Dorothy Walker Bush who lives in Greenwich, Connecticut, visits frequently.

President Bush and his mother, Dorothy Walker Bush, (left) greet the minister after church services in Florida. President Bush likes to fish and be outdoors.

President Bush likes to fish and to drive his speedboat. He often plays tennis with his family. He is active in the Episcopalian Church he attends. He jogs to keep fit and loves to eat Tex-Mex food.

When he was a boy, George Bush wanted to play major league baseball. Today, he is the "major league" leader of one of the most powerful nations on earth.

George Bush (left) in 1939

GEORGE HERBERT WALKER BUSH

1924   June 12—Born in Milton, Massachusetts, the second son of Prescott Bush and Dorothy Walker Bush

1942   Graduated from Phillips Academy in Andover, Massachusetts

1942   Enlisted in U.S. Navy

1942-45 Served as a U.S. Navy pilot in World War II

1945   January 6—married Barbara Pierce in Rye, New York

1948   Graduated from Yale University with degree in economics

1948   Moved to Texas

1953-59 Co-founder, Zapata Petroleum Corporation

1956-64 President, Zapata Offshore Company, Houston, Texas

1964   Republican candidate for U.S. Senate

1967-71 Served in the United States Congress from the Seventh District, Texas

1971-72 U.S. ambassador to the United Nations

1973-74 Chairman, Republican National Committee

1974-75 Chief U.S. Liaison Office, China

1976-77 Director, Central Intelligence Agency

1979   Campaigned for Republican primary nomination to U.S. presidency

1980   Became Ronald Reagan's running mate as vice president

1981-88 Vice president of the United States

1988   November 8—Elected president of the United States

1989   January 20—Inaugurated as 41st president of the United States

PHOTO CREDITS

AP/Wide World, Inc.—1, 3, 4, 5, 7 (right), 9 (top right), 19 (both), 20 (both), 21 (left), 23 (right), 25, 26, 28 (bottom), 29, 31 (left), 32

David Valdez, The White House—Cover, 2

Official Photograph The White House Washington—7 (left), 12, 30

Official U.S. Navy Photograph—10 (right), 11 (both)

Official White House Photograph—10 (left), 18

Midland Desk & Derrick Collection The Petroleum Museum, Midland, Texas—17

Phillips Academy—9 (bottom)

Courtesy Permian Historical Society Archival Collection, The University of Texas of the Permian Basin, Odessa, Texas—15

UPI/Bettmann Newsphotos—6, 21 (right), 22, 23 (left), 24, 27 (both), 28 (top left & right), 31 (right)

Yale University, Office of Public Information—13, 14

ABOUT THE AUTHOR

For the past 25 years June Behrens has been writing for children. Her many years as an educator have made her sensitive to the interests and needs of young readers. Mrs. Behrens has written over 60 books, touching on a wide range of subjects in both fiction and nonfiction. June Behrens received her academic education from the University of California at Santa Barbara, where she was honored as Distinguished Alumni of the Year for her contributions to the field of education. She has a Master's degree from the University of Southern California. Mrs. Behrens is listed in *Who's Who of American Women.* She lives with her husband in Rancho Palos Verdes, near Los Angeles.